My name is Eliza
and I don't talk at school

A storybook for children and a guidebook
for parents and professionals

Lucy Nathanson

ISBN 978-1-78808-442-0

Illustrator: Matthew Westwood
Editor: Carmel Edmonds

Acknowledgements

Thank you to everyone who has supported me in the process of creating this book.

To my mum, for teaching me to always be authentic and to follow my heart.

To my dad, who is no longer here, who showed me love when I was a little girl and gave me the middle name "Eliza".

To my sister Anna, for always being there for me and believing that I can achieve all I imagine, and for your amazing attention to detail when reviewing the proofs of this book.

To the real Mrs Davis, my nan, for your unwavering belief in me and for telling me as a child: "No matter what the result, if you try your best, I am proud of you".

To all of my friends for listening to my dreams and being patient when I continually sent illustrations for feedback.

To Lauren, someone who is always there to support me, make me laugh and cheer me on.

To Matthew Westwood, my fantastic illustrator, who saw my vision and brought Eliza and her story to life in pictures.

To Carmel Edmonds, for your kindness, time and patience when editing this book.

To the parents and the children who read the proofs of this book and gave feedback.

For the children with selective mutism I have had the pleasure to work with that inspire me every day.

Contents

How To Read This Book

The aim of this book is to help children with selective mutism to feel as though they are not alone, and to provide an avenue for parents and children to speak about their condition. (The use of "parents" throughout this book refers also to primary caregivers and guardians.) As selective mutism is a very sensitive issue, we need to be careful when presenting this book to children; when talking about their difficulties and fears explicitly, what we don't want to do is add to the child's anxiety level. Therefore, following the steps below is paramount. This book can be read on different levels – simply as a story book for children to read about a child who has similar fears to them, or as a tool to introduce some of the strategies in the book. Adults should be led by the child and therefore not push any of the strategies if the child is not ready.

Step 1: Read the book before presenting it to your child.

Decide whether this book is appropriate for your child. It is designed for children who are 6 years or older and are aware of their inability to talk in some situations.

Eliza explicitly talks about her inability to speak at school and her feelings. The explicit reference to Eliza's inability to talk is not appropriate for children below 6 years of age, as well as for children who are unaware of their difficulties with talking. If you feel your child is not ready for the story, you can still use the therapeutic approach shown in the story and explained on pages 9–12 to help your child with their selective mutism.

Step 2: Read the book with your child, or give the book to them to read.

Consider your child's reading ability and how you feel your child will react to the story.

- Do not mention that Eliza has the same difficulties as them.
- Talk about Anna and her fear of dogs. This offers a way of introducing the topic of facing fears in a way that's not directly about your child.
- If your child mentions that Eliza is like them, acknowledge this by agreeing – "Yes, you're right, she is" – and then move on to Step 3.

Step 3: Focus on how your child is braver than Eliza.

For example: "But you are braver than Eliza, you can talk to some friends at school!" or "You can talk in the shop!"

Step 4: Talk about the story, with a focus on Eliza – not on your child.

You can do this using the discussion questions on page 13, if you feel that this would be useful for your child.

Some children will not have a therapist like Lily (page 26) in their life. If your child asks about Lily, you could say something like, "Lily is a character in the book and she has taught us a lot – for example, that there are a lot of children all around the world who find it hard to talk at school". Lily's role in the book is to demonstrate stimulus fading in a clear and simple way.

Only move on to Step 5 after your child has read the book a few times and is enjoying the book. Do not initiate this step prematurely.

Step 5: Introduce the idea of trying some of the strategies in the book.

For example: "Maybe we could try having a brave chart like Eliza?" or "Maybe we could practise doing brave things like Eliza – but nothing too scary, just small baby steps, such as…" and give a suggestion that is easy for your child, based on your knowledge of what they can do.

> Reassure your child that they won't have to do anything too scary. Say that you will start with something easy and will move forward in baby steps. Give the impression that it will be fun to practise doing brave things. Remember to make a step smaller if it is too difficult for your child to achieve.

The Therapeutic Approach

Here, I explain how different parts of the story demonstrate the experience of selective mutism and the therapeutic approach in helping a child.

Page 20: People your child doesn't talk to

This section describes how Eliza feels with strangers. This also applies to people your child cannot talk to yet (such as family friends, grandparents, aunts and uncles, etc). It is best if these adults provide a friendly atmosphere, but do not focus too much on your child initially. Children with selective mutism do not enjoy being the centre of attention when they feel anxious, so the best approach is for those adults to say, "Hello Eliza, it's nice to see you," and then talk to the parent without focusing too much on the child.

Pages 26–29: Stimulus fading

These pages demonstrate stimulus fading (referred to as 'the sliding-in technique' by Johnson & Wintgens in *The Selective Mutism Resource Manual*). Stimulus fading is a behavioural technique used to help people to overcome phobias. The general principle is that first the person becomes desensitised to, or comfortable with, their phobia at a distance. The stimulus is then moved gradually closer, enabling the person to become comfortable with the stimulus as it comes nearer. For example, if a person has a phobia of snakes, we may begin with a snake in a cage 10 metres away from the person, and once they are comfortable with this, the cage and snake could be moved one meter closer to them, and so on. The idea is that the person always becomes comfortable with the current step before moving on to the next step.

When working with a child with selective mutism, we "fade in" a new person in the same way. The child with selective mutism plays and talks with a talking partner (usually the parent) until speech is established. The new person then enters the room for a moment and leaves. The new person re-enters and is busy in the background, avoiding eye contact with the child. The new person gradually moves closer once the child is comfortable at each step. Eventually the new person can sit next to the child and talking partner as they play, and then begin to join in the activity, starting to interact with the child. The eventual goal is that the child will be able to move from speaking only to the talking partner to talking with the new person.

When I start working with a child, I usually start with a home session that follows the procedure outlined on these pages.

Please keep in mind that speech is not necessarily achieved in the first session. The adult must move at the child's pace and only move forward a step if the child is comfortable at the current step. This can take multiple sessions. It is also important to add that although the talking partner (the parent in this case) is prompting for speech; from the child's perspective, the focus of these sessions should not be on talking but on playing games and having fun.

From my experience, stimulus fading is the quickest way for a child with selective mutism to talk to a new person. The procedure outlined can be recreated by therapists, teachers and new people to help the child to talk with them.

Page 30: Reassuring your child

This is the first step of therapy: reassuring the child that they can have a lot of fun without talking. This reassurance reduces the child's anxiety levels and paradoxically puts them in a stronger position to start talking.

Pages 32–34: Graded exposure in the community

In this part of the story, we see how parents of children with selective mutism can create opportunities for their child to practise facing their fears in small incremental steps.

It is imperative that you start by encouraging your child to do something they can already do and make the next step so tiny that it is barely noticeable. If the step is too big then the child may not be able to achieve it and they will lose confidence.

For example, if the goal is for the child to answer the shopkeeper, ensure that they are comfortable talking in front of the shopkeeper, firstly at a distance and then gradually getting closer over time and at their pace.

It will be for the parent to judge, depending on the age of the child and their awareness of their condition, whether it is best to do this overtly by discussing "practising being brave" or whether to encourage them to face their fears naturally within everyday situations without explicitly talking about it.

The approach taken depends on the individual child – there is not one approach that fits all children.

Page 32: Brave charts

This part of the story shows the use of a "brave chart". It is important to not make a big deal out of talking, but I have found that some children, especially younger children, respond well to the use of a brave chart. This is like a sticker chart but for being "brave". Every child is different; some will love it and some won't, so think about how your child would respond. Some parents have told me that their child has suddenly made strides forward after introducing a brave chart. However, this has to be done in the right way.

Some important points:

1. A brave chart should not be used as a bribery tool ("If you do this, then you'll get..."). This does not work and only adds pressure.

Reinforce *after* the child has achieved a new step, for example: "You were really brave today when you helped me with the shopping list in the shop, so let's add another star to your brave chart".

2. When guiding the child forward, make sure it is a baby step. Never prompt them to order their food before they can talk to you in the presence of people in public. They won't be able to do it, which will only lower their confidence. We want to always set the child up for success, and prompt the next achievable baby step.

3. I never use the words "talking" or "speaking" with the child – instead we are practising being brave, and being brave is not just about talking and speaking; being brave could be trying new things, taking part in an activity, going to after school club and so on.

From my experience, a brave chart can work beautifully with some children to spur them on but it has to be done in the right way and they have to enjoy the experience.

Page 34: Small steps

This part of the story mentions the need to make a step smaller if it is too difficult for your child to achieve. Making steps small enough so that your child can achieve them ensures that they experience a feeling of success. This will help them to continue to make strides forward.

Page 35: At school – explaining to other children

Here, we see how your child's teacher could talk to the class and explain to the other children how they should act when your child begins to talk. Again, such a class talk is not always necessary, especially not for younger children (less than 5 years of age).

If younger peers make comments such as "Why doesn't Eliza talk?" then it is advisable for the teacher to speak to them on a one-to-one basis and explain that your child will talk when they are ready, they shouldn't speak about the child not talking, and they should just act normally when the child does start talking.

From my experience, a whole class discussion is sometimes useful for children who are slightly older (6 years plus) and are aware of their difficulty, so may be concerned that peers will make comments if they start talking. If it is decided that a class discussion would be useful, do this without the child with selective mutism present.

Confident Children have made child-friendly videos explaining selective mutism that can be shown to the class. There is a video for younger children and a video for older children.

These videos can be accessed for free at www.confidentchildren.co.uk/videos.

Page 36: At school – small steps programme

Finally, this part of the story demonstrates how a simultaneous school-based small steps intervention can work, whereby the child begins to gradually face their fear of talking at school.

Small steps in the community and at school will allow the child to gradually start to achieve goals which were once thought not possible.

For more information on how to apply the techniques to your child, contact Confident Children via www.confidentchildren.co.uk

Discussion Questions

Here are some questions to discuss with the child about the story.
These discussion questions are optional.

1. What does Eliza find hard?

2. Did Eliza get braver by the end of the story? How do you know?

3. What helped Eliza get braver?

4. Do you think Eliza will be able to talk at school one day?

5. Do you think it is good that Mrs Davis spoke to the class?

6. How did Anna stop being scared of Buster?

My name is Eliza
and I don't talk at school
at school

A storybook for children
and a guidebook for parents
and professionals

LUCY NATHANSON
www.confidentchildren.co.uk

My name is Eliza and I don't talk at school. My teacher thinks I'm shy and so do lots of the children in my class – some people even think I can't talk! But...my mum knows that I CAN talk and I am NOT shy!

At home I use my voice lots and lots! I run around the house and sing and shout! I jump on the trampoline in my garden and call out loud: "Mum, look at me!"

I have got a friend called Anna and when she comes to my house she hears my voice a lot. We run around the house and garden, chasing after each other playing catch, giggling and giggling at the top of our voices!

But when I go to some places, like the shops, then I can't talk. I get a big worry feeling and it's like my voice gets stuck. It sometimes feels like there's a big, grey cloud.

If my worry feeling is really big, then my body gets stiff, like a statue. When this happens, my words can't come out.

Some people think that if they are super friendly and say, "Hello Eliza! How are you?" then I will answer, but when people speak to me, it makes it harder for me to talk! I like it better if they don't ask me questions; then my worry feeling gets smaller and I can talk to my mum in front of them.

I can sometimes even talk to strangers after a while, if they don't ask me any questions at the start, and my worry feeling gets even smaller.

I like going to school because I get to do Arts and Crafts. Art is my favourite lesson of all! I love drawing and painting and making things.

But my worry feeling is the biggest at school.

I've never spoken to my teacher, Mrs Davis. She is a really nice lady but I find it hard to talk to teachers. At school I wave at Mrs Davis when she calls my name in the register, and I have a toilet pass that I show her if I need to go to the toilet. I point at what I want for lunch so the dinner lady knows, and I nod and shake my head so grown-ups know what I want.

My friend Anna used to be scared of dogs.
I've got a dog called Buster so Anna used to
be very scared when she came to my house.
Mum suggested that we tie Buster up when
Anna came to play. Anna stopped being so
scared when she saw that Buster was tied
up. The next time Anna came, Mum asked her
if she'd like to touch Buster for one second.
Anna was very scared but one second didn't
seem like a long time, so she did it!

Anna said she wouldn't mind trying again, and this time she stroked him for five seconds. Anna said Buster felt soft and warm and she was happy that she stroked him – Buster looked happy too! Soon she stroked him for 10 seconds and then 20 seconds and guess what? Anna's not scared of Buster any more! When she comes to my house she loves playing with him!

Mum asked a lady called Lily to help me to talk. Lily's job is to help children who find it scary to talk!

Lily came to my house. At first I felt the worry feeling show up and I didn't really want her to come. But when Lily came, she didn't really talk to me. She said hello to my mum and told me it was nice to meet me, but then she went out of the living room. Mum and me carried on playing a game that I like called Guess Who? Maybe you know that game too?

After a while, Lily came back into the living room, but she didn't talk to me and then she went straight out again! Then she came back into the room, but this time she stayed; she sat on the sofa and she read a book. Lily must really like her book because she wanted to read it even when she came to my house!

Lily wasn't looking at me so I carried on playing Guess Who? with my mum – my worry feeling was getting smaller, because Lily wasn't listening, so I carried on talking to Mum. After a while Lily started to join in the game and the three of us played together. She even asked me some questions and I could answer because now my worry feeling was really small and my voice didn't get stuck!

Lily told me that lots and lots of children in countries all around the world find it scary to talk. There are children who find it hard to talk at school in England, America, Poland, Spain, Brazil, Australia and even more countries! I was so surprised because I thought I was the only child in the whole world who was scared to talk, but there are LOADS of children who can't talk at school!

Lily said there's no need to worry about talking for now because I can have lots of fun without talking!

Lily told my mum that to help me be brave and to make my worry feeling go away, I need to practise being brave. She said we won't practise doing really big scary things, just small baby steps. Like I could practise talking to my mum in the shop far away from the shopkeeper.

The next day we went to the shop and I practised talking to Mum when there was no one around. Mum put a star on my brave chart because I talked to her in the shop! Then the next day we tried again, but we went one step closer to the shopkeeper. The shopkeeper didn't even know I was practising being brave! And guess what? I got another star on my brave chart! When my brave chart gets filled up, then I'm going to get a prize!

I've been practising being brave lots, and
each time it gets less scary. If something
is too scary and my worry feeling is too
big, then Mum thinks of something easier
I can do that is still being brave. Right now,
ordering my food in a restaurant feels really
scary, so instead I tell Mum what food
I want when the waitress is quite close by.

At school, Mrs Davis told the children in
my class to just act normally when I start
talking and to not make a fuss about it. I'm
sure my friends will be really happy when
I start talking, but Mrs Davis has told them
to put their best acting hats on and when
I talk they are going to act like I always
talked! This makes me feel better.

I still don't talk all the time at school, but I have started doing a bit of talking – I have even played Guess Who? with Mum in a small room next to my classroom.

I wonder if you've been listening carefully
– do you remember my name? My name is
Eliza and every day I'm getting bigger and
braver. For now, there are lots of ways to
have fun without talking and I know that
soon, when I am ready, I will be able to talk
at school. Then EVERYONE will know that:
I am NOT shy!

The End

Made in the USA
Las Vegas, NV
12 September 2024

95165204R00024